TUTORING MATH: MY PHILOSOPHY AND APPROACH

TERESA M. O'BRIEN

TUTORING MATH: MY PHILOSOPHY AND APPROACH

TERESA M. O'BRIEN

Copyright © 2021 Teresa M. O'Brien
All rights reserved. This book or any portion thereof may not be reproduced or used in any manner whatsoever without the express written permission of the publisher except for the use of brief quotations in a book review.
Printed in the United States of America.

First printing, 2021.
ISBN: 978-1-7379432-0-4
Teresa M. O'Brien
O'Brien Consulting Group
Midland, MI 48640

DEDICATION

To all my students – past, present and future…and their parents

Table of Contents

INTRODUCTION 1
AN ENVIRONMENT TO REDUCE STUDENT STRESS 5
PROVIDING FEEDBACK 9
ADDRESSING THE LESSON OF THE DAY 13
FINDING MISSING OR INCOMPLETE FOUNDATIONAL MATH SKILLS 19
BRINGING THE STUDENT ONTO CENTERSTAGE 25
TUTORING ADULTS 27
TUTORING AND HUMILITY 29
HOW I AM A BETTER PERSON FOR HAVING BEEN A MATH TUTOR 33
WORD PROBLEMS 37

INTRODUCTION

In the summer between my freshman and sophomore year in college, I met with some of my classmates from high school. We were talking about our career choices and college majors. One of my classmates said she had thought about choosing a particular major but once she realized she would have to take a math class, she chose a different major, one that didn't require the math class. Another of our classmates said she had also changed her major for the same reason. This had shocked me at the time. Both were B+ students and should have been able to pass any one term of math. This stayed with me for decades.

When I retired from Dow, I decided I would have time to work with junior high and high school students so they would be able to do math well enough that they could choose the best college major for themselves and not have to sub-optimize their career choice.

I called the local school system and was directed to one of the junior high counselors who kept a list of tutors' names for distribution to teachers and parents throughout the Midland Public Schools.

Now, at this point, I have spent over 15 years tutoring math for 6 – 12th grades in Midland Public Schools. Sometimes I have stayed with students through high school graduation and other times just for a year or so. Over the years, I have found ways that work for me to help students and I wanted to pass them on to other math tutors.

I began with students in junior high first. I figured that I should easily be able to do that math. After a couple of years, I moved up to help all students in any grade. Since I didn't have a textbook to look at ahead of time, I was nervous about tutoring some of the math, especially the more advanced levels. But I have found that with notes the students have, what they DO know, their textbooks, and online help, we most always can figure out the work in real-time.

I think math is fun. It is almost like a different language. Once one cracks the code, math is far easier than most students think. I love helping students with learning math, not because I think they will become mathematicians or scientists, but because I want to expand their world of possibilities to do what they love. This is one fewer hurdle on their path to achievement.

While I, myself, love science (I have a bachelor's and master's degree in chemistry) that is not what I want for the students. I want them to pass math so they can complete their education and be contributors to society. I don't want them to be artificially limited or denied doing their hearts' desire because they couldn't pass the required math classes.

I help them see that they CAN do math and that they can ask for a tutor to help them through the tough spots. In fact, learning to ask for help and understanding isn't a sign of weakness or of shame and it is an important life skill. Sometimes our school system reinforces the concept that we rise or fall only on our own merit.

That's not the way that the world of business operates for success. Many times I have asked colleagues for help – either to bounce ideas off for improving clarity of thought or sometimes simply for information. This is part of what being a professional is all about. No one knows everything. What we need to know is how to find the answers to questions that we have. Sometimes we even need help in figuring out what questions to ask! One professor I had in college said that the most important skill he could impart to his students is to know how to go about the process of finding answers to questions (looking things up.)

I'm not sure how the students see me at first. But I do work to show them that I believe they can learn to do their math work. We dialogue and I treat them like I would a colleague that comes to my office for help. We talk about what the problem is and I ask questions that might help them develop the answer to the problem on their own.

If I tell them the answer is 16, they learn little. But if I start having them work through the problem and ask questions (with emphasis on certain words that are clues to where the answer lies) they start to figure out the solutions. I let them try to work it out, but I don't let them flounder.

It is a fine line between letting them have space to think and leaving them hanging when they don't know the answer. That takes practice to adjust to and it varies by student.

Some students think aloud as they process information and others think internally and then speak. Having been a facilitator of meetings for years has helped me hone this skill of knowing when to wait and when to talk. I still don't always get it right.

I have been working to help students not only get through their current math class but to believe that they can do the math. I want everyone to be able to choose the course of their life without worrying about one math class derailing them in college, as happened to a few of my high school classmates.

While I feel that there is no shame in asking for help, I also recognize that it is not my story to tell as to which students I am tutoring. That is their story. I respect their privacy. That is why I have put no names in this booklet, not even made-up ones.

QUESTION FOR REFLECTION:

What is your "why" for being a math tutor?

AN ENVIRONMENT TO REDUCE STUDENT STRESS

Usually, when I first meet with students, they are already at least halfway through the school term and are really struggling. At that point, the student equates math with STRESS.

So, I work to reduce the student's stress, while helping the student understand the lesson of the day. I also watch for underlying math knowledge that may be missing or incomplete. Patience and optimism have helped me as a tutor.

Often when I first start working with a student, they are somewhat distant and frightened. The students and parents are worried the student might flunk math in the current term. Parents have told me there have often been tears and yelling over doing math homework. Everyone is frustrated. (Parents usually tell me later that homework time in their house becomes much calmer after I start tutoring their child.) It is hard to learn when under stress.

I start by taking my cues from the student. After I introduce myself, I ask them to call me by my first name. I always try to sit *next* to them, so it feels as though we are on the same side. In the first session, I learn what their favorite class is (rarely math!) and what activities they like to do for fun. Just thinking about the answers to these questions reduces their stress a little.

Then I tell them that these sessions are all about their learning, not about me knowing. If I explain something and they don't understand it, they need to tell me so I can explain it differently, so they do understand. I tell them they can say: "Whoa!" or "The train went off the track here," or "You lost me," etc. Any of these will work.

Then, we start with the lesson of the day. I begin by asking what they didn't understand in the lesson. I ask the question in such a way as to set the expectation that there is something the student doesn't understand. This is a small way of giving them permission to open up. After we address any of those questions, we review the day's lesson and start working on problems.

Usually, after a few sessions, their terror of math and of me reduce enough that they smile when I walk into the room. I almost always ask them how the world of math is treating them? And how they are treating the world of math? It helps keep the fear away from them personally but tells me a lot about their progress. It is also a reminder to them that this is a two-way street.

I try to find things to laugh about (never directed at the student's performance.) Humor reduces stress – especially if I can turn the humor towards me.

I respect each student for where they are, and I honor them for where they are in the process of learning math. Each student has a different learning style and a way of processing information. As I have tried over the years to adapt my teaching to match their learning style, I have come to appreciate both the challenge for teachers to teach simultaneously so many different styles of learning and for the students to try to adapt to the teaching style of their teachers.

I tell every student when we first meet that we all learn in different ways. I try hard to teach them in ways that they can understand, based on their learning styles and interests, but I just might not be successful. It usually takes me a few weeks of meetings to get to know the student well enough to be able to understand how they learn and to figure out how to explain things in ways which make sense to them.

If after a few weeks they don't think that I am helping them, they are to ask their parent to find them another tutor. This is all about them learning.

I have learned over the years that when students say that a section of math is easy, that means they are getting it. I tell them that is "music to my ears."

While they may think it is just a platitude, it is the truth. It is one of the signs I look for that things are improving from the perspective of the student. Another one is that they smile when they see me.

QUESTION FOR REFLECTION:

What subjects stressed you in school? Did you have teachers who heightened or reduced that stress? What did they do?

PROVIDING FEEDBACK

As the student starts working on problems, I give lots of immediate feedback (yes, exactly, right, correct, good, perfect.) This helps remind the student that they DO know how to do a lot of the math, which is also a stress reducer/confidence builder.

When they make a mistake, I give them immediate feedback, as well. I rarely say "that's wrong" because that just builds stress. Instead, I say "let's think about that" or "uhhhh," or "ummmm." This gives the student a chance to pause and reflect on where they might need to change something. If they just made a simple mistake (e.g., transposed numbers), they can quickly fix it and move on. If this is something that they truly don't understand, I move into an explanation and a teaching moment.

When a student makes a mistake, I always include myself in the correction phrase – "let's think about that" – and when they get it right I give them full credit – "you did that perfectly" or "great job!" This helps share the burden and reinforce the success. In either case, the student gets immediate feedback and no sense of censure, which reduces stress.

When they are working on a problem that they aren't totally knowledgeable in solving, I say out loud how I am thinking through the problem. For example, if we are working to solve: $m-17=10$, then I would say:

1- Let's write out the equation (which the student does)
2- In the end, we want to have m equal a number, right?
3- Therefore, we need to get the numbers all on one side of the equal sign and the letter m on the other
4- So what should we do first?
5- Right! Let's move the -17 to the other side of the equal sign
6- If 17 is currently SUBTRACTED from m, then what do we have to do to "cancel out" or "get rid of" 17 from this side of the equation?
7- If we add 17 to THIS side of the equation, what do we have to do to have the equation stay in balance?
8- What do we do with the +17 and the +10?
9- What does m equal?

This starts to build the thought process in the students' heads. It gives them a basic framework to use in solving any problem once the equation is set up. Many times, students may have missed hearing this part in class as they became further behind in understanding math. As time goes on, I let them take the lead in asking questions and thinking through the process.

This is all about setting them up for success by giving them the tools to figure problems out on their own. By thinking out loud as they are doing the work, this further helps reinforce the process. We don't all learn the same way so seeing, hearing, and writing simultaneously can help to trigger learning and memory.

I am thrilled each time a student says that the lesson of the day was easy. Or, when I see them smiling during a session, or when they work out a problem all the way through on their own. I am happy for them because they are feeling a little better about themselves that day, and potentially they are more likely to choose a career that interests them, without limitation of any class they might have to take to get a degree.

One technique I have used with students who are really struggling in a class is after the first few weeks (usually 2 sessions per week in the beginning), I ask them to write down in their notebook at what time in the class they start to lose understanding of what the teacher is saying. Even before they see a big change in their test performance, they will start to understand more of the information being presented that day in class. Small wins are important, so I reinforce to the student that things are improving (independent of just my saying so.)

QUESTION FOR REFLECTION:

Which of these techniques will you try to encourage your student?

ADDRESSING THE LESSON OF THE DAY

As we continue to meet, I always ask the student at the beginning of the session if there is anything that they have had a question about since the last time we met. It is a good way to get them focused on math while addressing any overarching concerns they may have.

We discuss the information that the teacher has presented since the last session. This helps them remember and helps me know what they are working on since I don't have a copy of their books or lesson materials. (I ask that they take notes in class and not just listen to what the teacher is saying.) This usually only takes 5-10 minutes. We talk about anything that the student didn't understand in class and then we start working on problems. We spend most of our time together working on their homework for that day. This way the students can understand what the teacher is saying in the next class.

I spend time trying to simplify what they are working on to as basic a level as I can. We then build from there. I try to indicate where this information could be used in the "real world." This is important to students who often feel that much of the information is a waste of time.

I also point out to students that even though some (much?) of the math is not what <u>they</u> will use in "the real world," they are building an important skill – thinking logically. That can help keep them from being taken advantage of in the future.

I point out to them that in whatever sport interests them, there are many exercises that a person does during practice sessions that are never used in the game exactly that way, but those exercises improve athletes for the game. They appreciate that comment. I find this particularly useful with high school students who are taking more advanced math.

When the students are working on problems, I am able to see what they are consistently getting wrong. We spend time on those situations, even putting together a note sheet of key math information which they can refer to when they are working on problems on their own.

Typically, the biggest challenge for students is working through story problems. Part of it is intimidation/fear that they have developed towards story problems and part is just a lack of understanding on how to approach a story problem. Story problems are where the most stress reducer techniques are needed. This can often be the last area where students start to feel comfortable.

Here is the approach I have developed over the years to help students. I tell them that a story problem is first a story and second a problem. So, I have them read the story aloud (not worrying about the math aspects) and ask if they understand what the problem is about. Sometimes they don't so we discuss what the words mean. Then the student reads the problem aloud again. Now we start "parsing" or "breaking down" each part of the story and writing math expressions for each piece.

It can also be very helpful to the students to draw a simple picture of what the story is about. A simple rectangle or triangle with numbers on it can be enough to help them understand. Visual learners can much more easily understand, even with the simplest of diagrams.

At this point, students are feeling a little better. We then look at the question they are to answer and figure out what math we can use. We think about the day's lesson and figure out which equation we might be able to use to get to the answer. I give them a chance to find it/figure it out. If they don't see it, I then ask questions that might lead them to the solution. "We are being asked for a ratio here, right? Are ratios usually adding/subtracting or multiplying/dividing?" "What equation did we use today that was multiplying/dividing or that used ratios?"

This helps students to figure out what to ask as they address a problem and starts to give them more confidence about working through story problems.

It's always good to ask the students at the end of working the problem to check if the answer they have written actually answers the question in the problem. This is especially important in the higher grades, where the students will have multi-step problems and multiple answers to provide.

It is possible for students not to fear story problems anymore. I had one young student who when I first started working with her hated story problems (imagine tears.) But within 6 months she was fine with them. In fact one day she forgot to bring home her math book and notes (it happens from time to time). Her mother told her to call me to cancel that session, but she said it was okay because I would make up story problems she could work on. She liked doing story problems. Her mother asked who she was and what she had done with her daughter?

I prefer not to have a session last more than one hour. After the students are back on track with the lesson of the day, most sessions are 30-45 minutes. Final exam sessions can be longer (up to two hours) as we work through their practice test questions. I spend 1-2 minutes at the end of the session reviewing any key learning of the session and verifying the date and time of the next session.

After we have been working together for a few months, I suggest that one day a week they ask a question in class about something that confuses them. By then they are usually getting close to being caught up with the rest of the class. I tell them that it is likely that if they don't understand it, probably a third of the class doesn't either. By this time, they usually have seen an improvement in their quiz scores and are getting back their confidence.

Sometimes math problems are given that are intended to intimidate a student while trying to verify that the student understands the concept being taught. This can really throw a student who is already behind in math. So, we talk about how sometimes problems are made to look very complicated but usually will quickly be able to be simplified if we just apply some basic math to the equation.

We then start to look for common terms (e.g. $4mn^3$ on one side of the equation and $4mn^3$ on the other side of the equation, which will cancel out when combined.) Looking at the individual pieces rather than just focusing on the whole equation at once can reduce the terror. Also knowing that the problem has been written specifically to intimidate all students NOT just them, can make it easier for them to focus and arrive at the answer.

QUESTION FOR REFLECTION:

What steps could you take to guide a student in approaching a story problem?

FINDING MISSING OR INCOMPLETE FOUNDATIONAL MATH SKILLS

Usually, if a student has been receiving average grades all along, there are just a handful of underlying math concepts that need to be shored up. If students have been struggling with math for years, they often need even more guidance to get caught back up.

Not understanding how to correctly work the total problem or missing a fundamental math skill will result in an incorrect answer, even if the student understands the actual math concept being discussed in class.

Even if there are only a handful of underlying math skills that students don't have a complete grasp on, this can seriously bring down their grades. So, while we are working on the lesson of the day, I am also watching for underlying math mistakes that the student is consistently making.

They may have missed some very basic things such as keeping the equal signs lined up as you move from line to line in solving a problem. Sometimes I will write out the solution to one problem step by step so that they can see how it should look. The student can then use it as a model. I always talk through what I am writing and thinking. It is always about setting the student up for success.

I always assume that the student can learn to do each of the problems of the day and I just keep asking the students questions that will help them find what they need to be able to do so. I have learned over the years to ask the same questions multiple times with patience and no stress in my voice.

For example, in rearranging terms: "If 15 is ADDED to k and we want to move the 15 to the other side of the equation, what will we have to do to eliminate 15 from THIS side of the equation?" It can take some students a long time to make that connection, while other students get it fairly quickly. Patience is the key. I remind myself it isn't about what I know but what the STUDENT needs to learn. Eventually, they will start asking and correctly answering the question themselves.

Many students have difficulty remembering whether the result of multiplying or dividing numbers results in a positive or negative number. Often there is a chart such as the one below to help them see whether the result is positive or negative.

Positive	X	Positive	=	Positive
Positive	X	Negative	=	Negative
Negative	X	Positive	=	Negative
Negative	X	Negative	=	Positive

But the answers just don't seem to stick. So I have them look at the table differently.

+	x	+	=	+
+	x	-	=	-
-	x	+	=	-
-	x	-	=	+

It is the same information in both tables with the second one being in math symbols. Now I have them think of the lines in the negative and positive symbols as either sticks, or pencils, or pens, or index fingers. We then talk about taking two negative "sticks" and crossing them to form a positive plus sign.

We look at the last line of the table above that shows negative times a negative is a positive. After doing this several times, students learn that the number of negative terms is the key to determining whether the final answer will be positive or negative. If there are an odd number of negative terms that are being multiplied or divided, there will always be one negative sign that didn't get paired up. If there is one negative sign left over, the answer will be negative.

Therefore, the statement for them to remember is: if there are an odd number of negative terms that are being multiplied or divided, the answer is negative. Otherwise, the answer is positive. This isn't an exercise for them to UNDERSTAND why the answer is so, but to REMEMBER THE RULE.

I sometimes have students create a special sheet with rules for these foundational areas where they are having difficulties. This becomes their quick reference guide for math skills that <u>they specifically</u> need for their work. I don't think I ever found a student that needed to work on as many as 10 of these issues. Usually, it is just a few of them. So, it isn't long before the student can start to see their grade improve.

Another area that they often don't know is their times tables (math facts.) The 6, 7, and 8 tables seem to have been especially glossed over. This means that they will either have to learn them or input them into a calculator.

Another area that really challenges students is going from scientific notation to regular numbers. And the whole area of estimating numbers. They have a tough time realizing that the answer they just gave me from their calculator is off by 1-3 orders of magnitude.

I have found that constant reminders are needed for many students to write the units of measure in their math problems. I discuss with them how units of measure can be used to ensure that the problem is set up correctly (e. g. miles per hour, not hours per mile.) I also discuss how they could improve their test results by a few points if they included the units of measure in their work and in their answer.

QUESTION FOR REFLECTION:

Can you think of a situation where you created a reference sheet for yourself? What motivated you to do that?

Reflect on this statement: "It isn't about what I know but what the student needs to learn." How can you apply this statement to your tutoring?

BRINGING THE STUDENT ONTO CENTERSTAGE

I learned from one of my students the importance of framing discussions in terms of things that are of interest to them. This particular student had difficulty with completing story problems but if it was a chemistry word problem, he was immediately engaged and believed he could solve it – and he actually did!

That's when I realized that students who are having a hard time in math approach the situation the way you or I would if watching a play from the back row of the upper balcony. We are participating from a great distance. But if I start speaking about the situation in terms of something the students are interested in, they are immediately transported to the stage itself. They have a frame of reference that they understand. This gives them a leg up in their willingness and ability to solve the problem.

For example, if the story problem is about figuring out the amount of lumber that a gardener needs to put a box garden in the backyard, change the location to the edge or front entrance of the local soccer field. Or explain where a concept that is being learned could be applied to something that is of interest to the student. Once again, this transports the student to center stage.

For example, problems around circles and triangles can be applied to patterns of movements in many sports. It's not that every situation can be applied to their particular sport but being able to do so even once a session will help them stay engaged and reminds them that this information has real-world applicability. This also gives them a comfortable reference point, which reduces their stress.

QUESTION FOR REFLECTION:

How do you create mental breaks for yourself when you are learning something new?

Note two situations where you have used math recently in your everyday life you could share with your student.

TUTORING ADULTS

I have had limited experience with tutoring adults. They break into two categories: college students and those who are in the workforce and want to improve basic math skills. But a couple of things that I have learned from my experience is that adults have a reason that they are working on improving their math skills. Having problems and assignments around the desired type of math is important to them.

Finding learning materials that address those types of problems is the next hurdle. Since the Internet now has lots of problems for free to choose from, this is just a matter of searching for the desired problems.

If the adult wasn't in a class, then I had to spend more time at the beginning of the tutoring session teaching the lesson that is being worked on because the student wasn't as familiar with the material.

If the adult students aren't part of an ongoing math class, then it is incumbent upon the tutor to give them some problems to work on before the next session, if the student has time and interest in doing self-learning between sessions.

Applying math to their everyday life, especially addressing why they wanted to learn some math, is critical. Staying focused on their purpose is important and creating word problems around situations that they are interested in is just as important for adults as it is for children.

My limited experience is that, initially, they are not confident enough in their skill to attempt problems on their own between sessions. Or, they don't feel they have the time to devote. This doesn't mean they don't want to learn. They just will learn at a slower pace.

As they get more comfortable, you can then try to give them a FEW problems between sessions. Adult lives are usually very busy so even 1-5 problems may be difficult for them to find the time to solve.

And it isn't always just the time. Spending time working on those problems can be a painful reminder of how far they have to go, especially when they are working on the problems on their own. So, patience is the key. And praise is just as important for adults as children – maybe more so. They aren't just learning a new skill; they may also be changing their perception of themselves. And perhaps changing others' perception of them. I appreciate the bravery and honesty that it takes for an adult to say that they can't do math but want to learn.

QUESTION FOR REFLECTION:

How is tutoring an adult in math different than a child? How is it similar?

TUTORING AND HUMILITY

Sometimes the textbooks use terms that I am not familiar with, so we look in the book or the student's notes to read what it means, or else I look it up on my phone. I think it is important for students to see that looking up something I don't know off the top of my head is acceptable. It gives them a chance to see that it is okay to say, "I don't know."

It also gives them a pattern of behavior to show how to figure out what something means. Several times I have had the students lean over and ask to use my phone to help me search faster for the answer (I am not the fastest typist) or to read the answer out loud for both of us. This helps them be actively involved in the learning process.

When we do find the answer, we read it aloud, then discuss how that applies to our given situation. I let the student lead in that discussion as much as possible. This gives them a chance to think through the information and digest it. It also gives them an important life skill. Not knowing something is not an excuse for stopping and doing nothing. It just means that it is time to do research to find the answer.

When I was teaching college classes, I would often see students just stop when they didn't know how to proceed, rather than asking others for help or doing some research themselves to find the answer. My math students will be better prepared.

Some of the bigger challenges for me have been the kinesthetic learners. It does help that they are writing things down. Sometimes they just need something to fiddle with (pencil, fidget, etc.) to help them focus. I have also cut out geometric shapes for them to handle. I am not very skilled with learning tools for this group but I do try to give them more short breaks in the sessions so they can reenergize for learning again. Moving around a bit can help them refocus.

Because there are so many types of calculators, I don't try to learn how to use their calculators; that is their responsibility. But I do work the problem in my head while they are entering the data into a calculator, so I know if they are reaching the correct answer.

I learned I don't need to know everything about math in order to tutor it. I just need to be willing to admit what I don't know and then look up the information in real-time and learn it well enough to help the student through the assignment.

I would encourage anyone who is thinking about tutoring math to give it a try. Start with the grades that you feel comfortable with and work your way up to higher grades. It is more than okay for a student to see that you have to look up something from time to time. They will just think to themselves that this was so hard that even my tutor didn't know the answer off the top of her head. When they figure it out, they will feel a sense of pride that they now know how to do something that their tutor had to look up to figure it out! What an ego boost for them!

Of course, that doesn't mean that we should be looking up EVERYTHING! But having them dig through their notes or search using the table of contents or index at the back of the book to find what we are looking for is an important skill for them to have when I am not there to help them look up something. It is also another way to reinforce active learning.

The students will look at the information that they have found and then have to decide whether that information is what we are looking for to solve our problem. That is an important critical thinking skill they are developing. They are learning by doing, which can be self-reinforcing for them.

QUESTION FOR REFLECTION:

What is your greatest fear about tutoring math?

HOW I AM A BETTER PERSON FOR HAVING BEEN A MATH TUTOR

One teacher of some of the students I have tutored said that the one thing I give the students is the belief that they CAN do the math. What a gift she gave me with that statement! It really changed my perspective. It wasn't just the lesson of the day they were learning; it was their perception of themselves that they were changing.

I had figured they could do math and hadn't really internalized that they believed they couldn't do math, only that they were having difficulty with it! WOW! I was shocked and thrilled. Since math had always come easily to me, it hadn't influenced my perception of myself, only of the subject itself. I hadn't considered that it might have influenced others' perceptions of themselves.

It has brought me great joy and satisfaction to see young people start to believe in their ability to do math. It reminds me that when I believe in someone else and act on that belief, that person's vision of himself/herself can also be changed.

Over the years, my sense of what I have been doing has broadened. I no longer look at these hours as just helping students to learn math. Of course, I am doing that. But now I see and feel I am opening up a whole additional world of possibilities for them.

For example, one girl that I tutored for just a semester learned that people are willing to help you if you just ask. When one of her friends was having trouble with a different subject in school, she told her friend to get a tutor. "There are people who are willing to help you if you just ask." What a tremendous lesson for her to learn at such a young age!

A young person's image can change by being able to do math. One young boy had been flunking math for a few years after a bad experience with one math teacher, even though he had done well in math previously. After working together for a year and a half, he turned his math grade back to an A. I couldn't have been prouder of him.

When I asked one high school senior that I hadn't worked with for a while, what his favorite class was, he thought about it for a minute, then said math – because it was <u>easy</u>!

One time I had a student that I was tutoring meet the next day with a couple of his friends that were in his math class to teach them what he had learned from me. This was a great way to reinforce his learning and also to help his two friends.

Another student told me that when I am there with him, he can do math. That is an important start.

I sometimes become part of their extended families. I have been invited to high school graduation parties for some who I have spent years helping. What a joy for me. I enjoy working with the students so much that it is the mental bar that I use to determine other volunteer work to participate in.

The students bring me such joy and hope for the world. Their worlds of possibilities aren't going to be limited by the fear of taking one math class in college. The world is a brighter place for all of us as these students follow their dreams.

It has been an absolute joy to help set these students up for success in life! I know the world is a better place for having so many improved contributors. I thank each of them for finding me and bringing so much joy and laughter into my life. They are all treasures to me, and I am so proud of all of them for having worked through their struggles and frustrations to achieve success in their math classes. Their openness and courage in overcoming their struggles with math humble me. It allows me to be more open and vulnerable myself. I have truly been blessed.

QUESTION FOR REFLECTION:

How can tutoring change you?

WORD PROBLEMS

This section is for parents who are helping their children with their math homework and for people who are just starting out as tutors. Here are three-word problems worked out in their entirety to show the thought process. It is important to not combine steps initially until students become more capable.

You can see how I approach word problems in detail. Giving students a structure for solving word problems allows them to have a greater chance of solving them. There are also many online resources to help you and the student work through a variety of problems.

Sample word problem (early geometry)

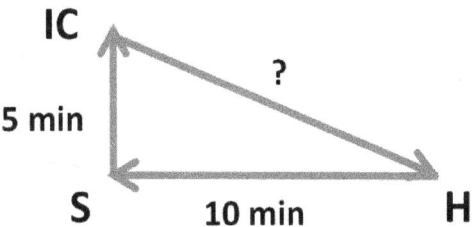

It took Mark ten minutes to walk west from his home to school in the morning, walking at a constant pace. After school, he walked at the same pace due north for five minutes to the ice cream store. If he walked at the same pace in a straight line from the ice cream store to his house, how long would it take him to walk home?

Step 1: Student reads the problem aloud
Step 2: Student explains the problem to me
Step 3: Student draws a picture of the story, adding in given information (times and locations)
Step 4: Student looks at the information that we have and what we are being asked for.
Step 5: Student determines what equation could be used to solve this situation (length of the side of a right triangle).
    Pythagorean Theorem ($a^2 + b^2 = c^2$)
Step 6: Student writes out equation:
$$a^2 + b^2 = c^2$$
Step 7: Student inserts information:
$$(10 \text{ min})^2 + (5 \text{ min})^2 = c^2$$
Step 8: Student works math on left side:
$$100 \text{ min}^2 + 25 \text{ min}^2 = c^2$$
Step 9: Student combines terms on left
$$125 \text{ min}^2 = c^2$$
Step 10: To solve for c, student takes the square root of both sides $\sqrt{125 \text{ min}^2} = \sqrt{c^2}$
$$11.2 \text{ minutes} = c$$
Step 11: Student rereads question to verify we have completely solved the problem
    It will take 11.2 minutes to walk home.

Sample Word Problem (early algebra)

Four years ago, Jane's age was half the age she will be in 12 years. How old is she now?

Step 1: Student reads the problem aloud

Step 2: Student explains the problem to me
Step 3: Student determines what we are solving for: Jane's age now
Step 4: Student assigns the letter J to Jane's age now
Step 5: Student breaks down the information in the problem;
    Jane's age 4 years ago: $J - 4$
    Jane's age in 12 years: $J + 12$
Step 6: Student combines all of information into one equation
$$J - 4 = \tfrac{1}{2}(J + 12)$$
Step 7: Student distributes the ½ across both terms in the parentheses
$$J - 4 = \tfrac{1}{2} J + (\tfrac{1}{2} \times 12)$$
$$J - 4 = \tfrac{1}{2} J + 6$$
Step 8: Student rearranges terms so the numbers are on one side and the letters on the other side of the equal sign (using math concept of doing opposite operation to remove something from one side of equation to the other)
$$J - 4 + 4 = \tfrac{1}{2} J + 6 + 4$$
$$J = \tfrac{1}{2} J + 10$$
$$J - \tfrac{1}{2} J = \tfrac{1}{2} J - \tfrac{1}{2} J + 10$$
$$\tfrac{1}{2} J = 10$$
Step 9: Since J is divided by 2, the student multiplies both sides by 2 so we can solve for J
$$2 (\tfrac{1}{2} J) = 2 (10)$$
$$J = 20$$
Step 10: Student rereads the question to verify we have answered the question
    Jane is currently 20 years old.

**Sample Word Problem
(more advanced geometry)**

A rectangle is 9 times as long as it is wide. If the length is increased by 9 inches and the width is decreased by 1 inch, the area will be 72 square inches. What were the dimensions of the original rectangle?

Step 1: Student reads the problem aloud.
Step 2: Student explains the problem to me.
Step 3: Student assigns letters to the variables.
    W = width of original rectangle
    L = length of original rectangle
Step 4: Student draws and labels original rectangle.
Step 5: Student writes relationship of width and length of original rectangle.
    L = 9W

```
┌─────────────────┐
│                 │
│    72 in²       │  W-1
│                 │
└─────────────────┘
       9W+9
```

Step 6: Student draws and labels new rectangle.
Step 7: Student writes length of new rectangle in terms of original rectangle width
    L + 9 = 9W + 9
Step 8: Student looks at the information that we have and what we are being asked for.
Step 9: Student determines what equation could be used to solve this situation (area of rectangle.)

Area = Length x Width (A = L x W)

Step 10: Student summarizes known information about new rectangle (in terms of W – so we have only one variable in the equation.)

$$(9W + 9 \text{ inches})(W - 1 \text{ inch}) = 72 \text{ inches}^2$$

Step 11: Student FOILS (distributes across the terms)

$$9W^2 - 9W \text{ inch} + 9W \text{ inch} - 9 \text{ inches}^2 = 72 \text{ inches}^2$$
$$9W^2 - 9 \text{ inches}^2 = 72 \text{ inches}^2$$

Step 12: Student moves $- 9in^2$ to other side of equation

$$9W^2 - 9 \text{ inches}^2 + 9 \text{ inches}^2 = 72 \text{ inches}^2 + 9 \text{ inches}^2$$
$$9W^2 = 81 \text{ inches}^2$$

Step 13: Since W^2 is multiplied by 9, the student divides both sides of equation by 9

$$(9/9) W^2 = (81/9) \text{ inches}^2$$
$$W^2 = 9 \text{ inches}^2$$

Step 14: Student takes square root of both sides of equation

$$\sqrt{W^2} = \sqrt{9 \text{ inches}^2}$$
$$W = 3 \text{ inches}$$

Step 15: Student calculates the length of original rectangle

$$L = 9W$$
$$L = 9 (3 \text{ inches}) = 27 \text{ inches}$$

Step 16: Student answers question

Length = 27 inches
Width = 3 inches

www.ingramcontent.com/pod-product-compliance
Lightning Source LLC
Chambersburg PA
CBHW072210100526
44589CB00015B/2459